CRUMBLES

over 30 sweet & savoury recipes

SABRINA FAUDA-RÔLE
PHOTOGRAPHY BY AKIKO IDA

hardie grant books

CONTENTS

TIPS

THE PRINCIPLES

A combination of fruit or vegetables, gently stewed and caramelised with a rich topping, which partly melts into the filling. A successful crumble is one in which a perfect balance is created between the crunchy topping and the caramelised filling.

FILLING

APPLES

Reliable choices are garden apples, King of the Pippins, or Golden Delicious. These have a good balance between sweetness and acidity and keep a firm texture on cooking. For a more purée-like consistency, choose Chantecler or Canadian Reinette russet. For a sharper flavour, go for Granny Smith.

OTHER FRUIT

Where possible, choose seasonal fruit, although frozen fruit can be a good alternative. Remember that frozen fruit will produce more juice than fresh fruit so sprinkle it with a little cornflour (cornstarch) before baking. Do not defrost frozen fruit before use.

VEGETABLES

Vegetables often need to be pre-cooked to reduce them to a purée or to bring out their flavour. If you are using frozen vegetables, allow to defrost before use.

CRUMBLE

CRUMBLE TOPPING

Three simple ingredients: butter, sugar and flour. Proportions will vary according to the recipe, to give a more or less crumbly or crunchy result. The process: lightly rub in the butter with the other ingredients using your fingertips until you have the consistency of rough breadcrumbs. Do not knead or over-mix the topping, otherwise it will become tough. Chill the crumble mixture while you prepare the filling: this will result in a better crumble. With a savoury crumble, you can add other ingredients to make it crisper: an egg, grated cheese, nuts, crumbled biscuits or crackers, etc.

FLOUR

You can choose a flour containing some bran, or wholemeal (whole-wheat) flour (for savoury crumbles) or use plain white spelt flour. Alternatively, use a mix of flours such as buckwheat, chestnut or maize.

BUTTER

Butter should be cold and cut into small chunks. Use a salted butter in sweet crumbles to counterbalance the sweetness of the fruit. Alternatively, use coconut oil. For savoury crumbles, use olive oil.

SUGAR

Unrefined cane sugar is the best option as it gives the crumble a nice crunch and a caramelised flavour. Otherwise, use granulated (raw) white sugar or soft brown sugar.

OPTIONAL EXTRAS

FLAVOURING THE CRUMBLE

In sweet crumbles, add nuts, cocoa, matcha powder, citrus zest, spices, praline, etc. In savoury crumbles, add spices, herbs, diced cheese, etc.

BUTTERING THE DISH

With sweet crumbles, you can butter the dish in which the fruit is to be cooked (especially if it is not non-stick). For an even more caramelised result, you might want to dust it with a spoonful of sugar.

ONE-DISH OR INDIVIDUAL CRUMBLES

All the recipes can be made in a large gratin dish or small ramekins. If choosing small ramekins, reduce the cooking time by one third.

CLASSIC APPLE
crumble

Preparation: 15 minutes
Cooking time: 45 minutes
Serves 6

CRUMBLE

120 g (4½ oz/1 cup) plain
  (all-purpose) flour
100 g (3½ oz/½ cup) unrefined
  cane sugar
100 g (3½ oz/scant ½ cup) cold
  salted butter, cubed

FRUIT

1.5 kg (3 lb 5 oz) apples

Preheat the oven to 180°C (350°F/Gas 4). Put the flour, sugar and butter into a bowl. Rub the butter into the other ingredients rapidly with your fingertips until the mixture resembles breadcrumbs. Chill.

Peel the apples, quarter them and remove the pips. Cut each quarter in three.

Arrange the chunks of apple in a gratin dish and sprinkle with the crumble. Bake in the oven for approximately 45 minutes, until the crumble is golden.

Ideal serving temperature: warm
Serve with double (heavy) cream

SUMMER FRUIT
crumble

Preparation: 10 minutes
Cooking time: 30 minutes
Serves 6

CRUMBLE
150 g (5½ oz/1 cup) plain (all-purpose) flour
100 g (3½ oz/½ cup) unrefined cane sugar
50 g (1¾ oz/½ cup) ground almonds (almond meal)
120 g (4½ oz/½ cup) cold salted butter, cubed

FRUIT
500 g (1 lb 2 oz/3½ cups) strawberries
250 g (9 oz/2 cups) raspberries
250 g (9 oz/2 cups) redcurrants
or
1 kg (2 lb 3 oz/8 cups) frozen mixed red fruits

Preheat the oven to 180°C (350°F/Gas 4). Put the flour, sugar, ground almonds and butter into a bowl. Rub the butter into the other ingredients rapidly with your fingertips until the mixture resembles breadcrumbs. Chill.

Rinse and hull the strawberries, and cut any larger ones in two. Rinse the raspberries. If using fresh fruits, rinse the redcurrants and discard their stalks.

Arrange the fruit in a gratin dish and sprinkle with the crumble. Bake in the oven for approximately 30 minutes, until the crumble is golden.

Ideal serving temperature: warm
Serve with double (heavy) cream

APRICOT AND PISTACHIO
crumble

Preparation: 15 minutes
Cooking time: 40 minutes
Serves 6

CRUMBLE
120 g (4½ oz/¾ cup) plain
  (all-purpose) flour
100 g (3½ oz/½ cup) unrefined
  cane sugar
100 g (3½ oz/1 cup) ground
  pistachios or finely chopped
  pistachios
100 g (3½ oz/scant ½ cup) cold
  salted butter, cubed

FRUIT
1.5 kg (3 lb 5 oz/8 cups) apricots

Preheat the oven to 180°C (350°F/Gas 4). Put the flour, sugar, pistachios and butter into a bowl. Rub the butter into the other ingredients rapidly with your fingertips until the mixture resembles breadcrumbs. Chill.

Rinse and dry the apricots. Cut them in half and remove the stones.

Arrange the apricot halves in a gratin dish and sprinkle with the crumble. Bake in the oven for approximately 40 minutes, until the crumble is golden.

Ideal serving temperature: warm
Serve with vanilla or pistachio ice cream

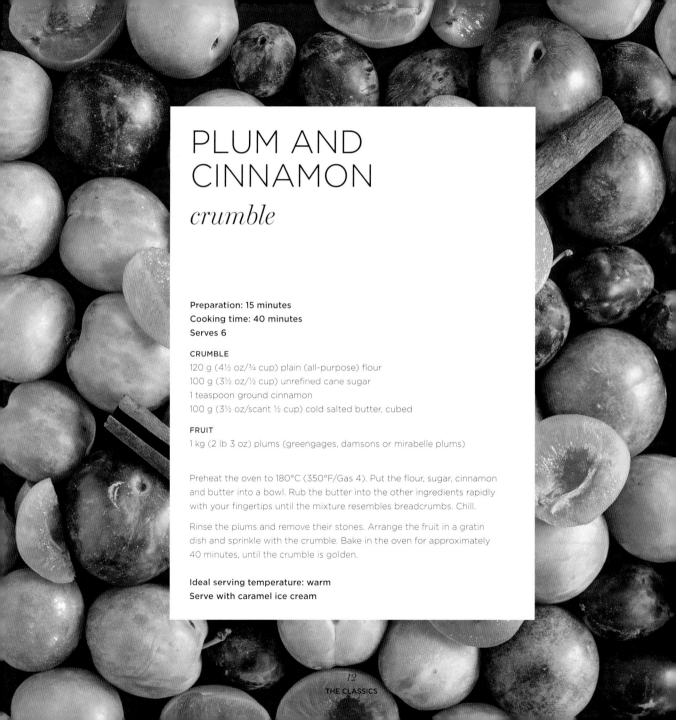

PLUM AND CINNAMON

crumble

Preparation: 15 minutes
Cooking time: 40 minutes
Serves 6

CRUMBLE
120 g (4½ oz/¾ cup) plain (all-purpose) flour
100 g (3½ oz/½ cup) unrefined cane sugar
1 teaspoon ground cinnamon
100 g (3½ oz/scant ½ cup) cold salted butter, cubed

FRUIT
1 kg (2 lb 3 oz) plums (greengages, damsons or mirabelle plums)

Preheat the oven to 180°C (350°F/Gas 4). Put the flour, sugar, cinnamon and butter into a bowl. Rub the butter into the other ingredients rapidly with your fingertips until the mixture resembles breadcrumbs. Chill.

Rinse the plums and remove their stones. Arrange the fruit in a gratin dish and sprinkle with the crumble. Bake in the oven for approximately 40 minutes, until the crumble is golden.

Ideal serving temperature: warm
Serve with caramel ice cream

STRAWBERRY AND RHUBARB
crumble

Preparation: 15 minutes
Cooking time: 30 minutes
Serves 6

CRUMBLE
120 g (4½ oz/¾ cup) plain
  (all-purpose) flour
100 g (3½ oz/½ cup) unrefined
  cane sugar
100 g (3½ oz/scant ½ cup) cold
  salted butter, cubed
1 vanilla pod

FRUIT
500 g (1 lb 2 oz) fresh or frozen
  rhubarb
500 g (1 lb 2 oz/3½ cups)
  strawberries

Preheat the oven to 180°C (350°F/Gas 4). Put the flour, sugar and butter into a bowl. Split the vanilla pod lengthwise and scrape out the seeds with the tip of a knife. Add the seeds to the bowl (reserving the pod). Rub the butter into the other ingredients rapidly with your fingertips until the mixture resembles breadcrumbs. Chill.

If using fresh rhubarb, rinse it then cut into sections of 1 –2 cm (½–¾ in). Otherwise, use frozen pieces without defrosting. Rinse and hull the strawberries, and cut any larger ones in half.

Arrange the fruit and the reserved vanilla pod in a gratin dish. Sprinkle with crumble and bake in the oven for approximately 30 minutes, until the crumble is golden.

Ideal serving temperature: warm
Serve with double (heavy) cream

BLACKCURRANT AND COFFEE
crumble

Preparation: 15 minutes
Cooking time: 20 minutes
Serves 6

CRUMBLE

120 g (4½ oz/¾ cup) plain
   (all-purpose) flour
80 g (2¾ oz/⅓ cup) unrefined
   cane sugar
100 g (3½ oz/¾ cup) crushed
   walnuts
1 tablespoon instant coffee
80 g (2¾ oz/⅓ cup) cold salted
   butter, cubed

FRUIT

500 g (1 lb 2 oz/5 cups)
   blackcurrants (fresh, frozen
   or tinned)
1½ teaspoons vanilla sugar
200 ml (7 fl oz) double (heavy)
   cream
2 tablespoons instant coffee

Preheat the oven to 200°C (400°F/Gas 6). Put the flour, sugar, walnuts, coffee and butter into a bowl. Rub the butter into the other ingredients rapidly with your fingertips until the mixture resembles breadcrumbs. Chill.

If using fresh blackcurrants, rinse and dry them. Drain tinned blackcurrants or use frozen ones as they are.

Mix the blackcurrants with the vanilla sugar in a bowl. Arrange half the sweetened blackcurrants at the bottom of 6 ramekins, then pour the cream on top. Sprinkle with coffee and finish with a second layer of blackcurrants. Sprinkle with the crumble. Bake in the oven for about 20 minutes, until the crumbles are golden.

Ideal serving temperature: cold
Serve with whipped cream

STRAWBERRY AND PEACH
crumble

Preparation: 10 minutes
Cooking time: 30 minutes
Serves 6

CRUMBLE
100 g (3½ oz/⅔ cup) plain (all-purpose) flour
100 g (3½ oz/½ cup) unrefined cane sugar
50 g (1¾ oz/½ cup) rolled (porridge) oats, barley or wheat flakes
125 g (4½ oz/½ cup) cold salted butter, cubed

FRUIT
500 g (1 lb 2 oz/3½ cups) strawberries
700 g (1 lb 9 oz) peaches or nectarines
1 teaspoon ground cardamom

Preheat the oven to 180°C (350°F/Gas 4). Put the flour, sugar, oats and butter into a bowl. Rub the butter into the other ingredients rapidly with your fingertips until the mixture resembles breadcrumbs. Chill.

Rinse and hull the strawberries, and cut any larger ones in half. Rinse and cut the peaches into eighths, removing the stones. Arrange the fruit in a gratin dish, then sprinkle with cardamom and top with the crumble. Bake in the oven for approximately 30 minutes, until the crumble is golden.

Ideal serving temperature: hot
Serve with vanilla ice cream

CREAMY APPLE
crumble

Preparation: 20 minutes
Cooking time: 40 minutes
Serves 6

CRUMBLE
100 g (3½ oz/⅔ cup) plain
   (all-purpose) flour
100 g (3½ oz/½ cup) unrefined
   cane sugar
100 g (3½ oz/generous 1 cup)
   flaked (slivered) almonds
100 g (3½ oz/scant ½ cup) cold
   salted butter, cubed

FRUIT
1 kg (2 lb 3 oz) apples
3 eggs
150 ml (5 fl oz) milk
150 ml (5 fl oz) single
   (pouring) cream
1½ teaspoons vanilla sugar

Preheat the oven to 180°C (350°F/Gas 4). Put the flour, sugar, flaked almonds and butter into a bowl. Rub the butter into the other ingredients rapidly with your fingertips until the mixture resembles breadcrumbs. Chill.

Peel the apples. Quarter them, remove the pips then cut each quarter in three.

Beat the eggs in a bowl with the milk, cream and vanilla sugar. Arrange the pieces of apple in a gratin dish, pour in the egg mixture and sprinkle with the crumble. Bake in the oven for approximately 40 minutes, until the crumble is golden.

Ideal serving temperature: warm
No accompaniment necessary

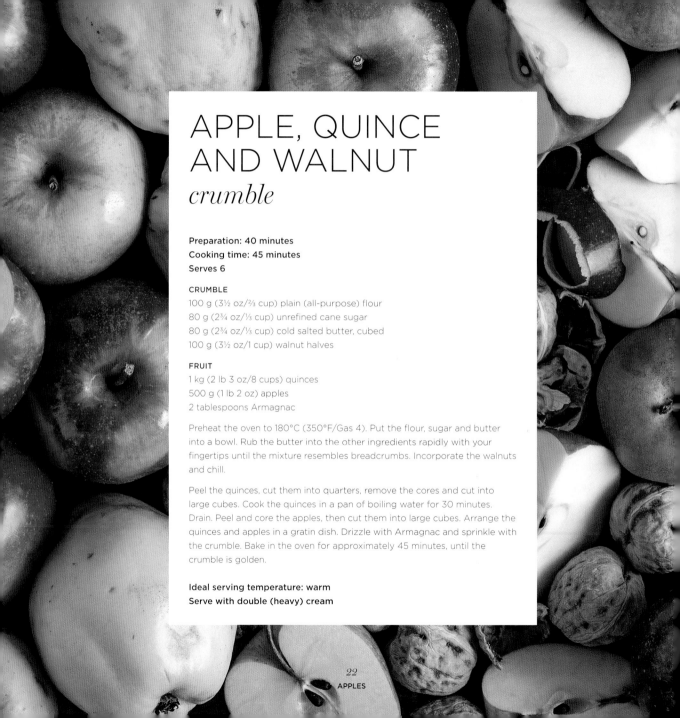

APPLE, QUINCE AND WALNUT
crumble

Preparation: 40 minutes
Cooking time: 45 minutes
Serves 6

CRUMBLE
100 g (3½ oz/⅔ cup) plain (all-purpose) flour
80 g (2¾ oz/⅓ cup) unrefined cane sugar
80 g (2¾ oz/⅓ cup) cold salted butter, cubed
100 g (3½ oz/1 cup) walnut halves

FRUIT
1 kg (2 lb 3 oz/8 cups) quinces
500 g (1 lb 2 oz) apples
2 tablespoons Armagnac

Preheat the oven to 180°C (350°F/Gas 4). Put the flour, sugar and butter into a bowl. Rub the butter into the other ingredients rapidly with your fingertips until the mixture resembles breadcrumbs. Incorporate the walnuts and chill.

Peel the quinces, cut them into quarters, remove the cores and cut into large cubes. Cook the quinces in a pan of boiling water for 30 minutes. Drain. Peel and core the apples, then cut them into large cubes. Arrange the quinces and apples in a gratin dish. Drizzle with Armagnac and sprinkle with the crumble. Bake in the oven for approximately 45 minutes, until the crumble is golden.

Ideal serving temperature: warm
Serve with double (heavy) cream

APPLE AND CHESTNUT
crumble

Serves 6
Preparation: 25 minutes
Cooking time: 30 minutes

CRUMBLE
60 g (2 oz/generous ⅓ cup)
  plain (all-purpose) flour
60 g (2 oz/⅔ cup) chestnut flour
80 g (2¾ oz/⅓ cup) unrefined
  cane sugar
100 g (3½ oz/scant ½ cup) cold
  salted butter, cubed

FRUIT
1 kg (2 lb 3 oz) apples
120 g (4½ oz) chestnut purée

Preheat the oven to 200°C (400°F/Gas 6). Put the flours, sugar and butter into a bowl. Rub the butter into the other ingredients rapidly with your fingertips until the mixture resembles breadcrumbs. Chill.

Peel and core the apples, and cut them into thin slices.

Put the chestnut purée in the bottom of 6 ramekins. Cover with apple slices and sprinkle with the crumble. Bake in the oven for approximately 30 minutes, until the crumbles are golden.

Ideal serving temperature: cold
Serve with whipped cream

APPLE, PECAN AND MAPLE
crumble

Preparation: 25 minutes
Cooking time: 25 minutes
Serves 6

CRUMBLE
120 g (4½ oz/¾ cup) plain
  (all-purpose) flour
80 g (2¾ oz/⅓ cup) unrefined
  cane sugar
100 g (3½ oz/scant ½ cup) cold
  salted butter, cubed
100 g (3½ oz/1 cup) pecans

FRUIT
1.5 kg (3 lb 5 oz) apples
2 knobs of butter
120 ml (4 fl oz) maple syrup

Preheat the oven to 180°C (350°F/Gas 4). Put the flour, sugar and butter into a bowl. Rub the butter into the other ingredients rapidly with your fingertips until the mixture resembles breadcrumbs. Incorporate the pecans and chill.

Peel and core the apples, then cut into large cubes. Melt the butter in a frying pan with the maple syrup. Add the apples and allow them to caramelise for 10 minutes.

Arrange the caramelised apples in a gratin dish and sprinkle with the crumble. Bake in the oven for approximately 25 minutes, until the crumble is golden.

Ideal serving temperature: warm
Serve with whipped cream and maple syrup

APPLE, GRAPE AND MATCHA
crumble

Preparation: 20 minutes
Cooking time: 40 minutes
Serves 6

CRUMBLE
120 g (4½ oz/¾ cup) plain (all-purpose) flour
100 g (3½ oz/½ cup) unrefined cane sugar
50 g (1¾ oz/½ cup) ground almonds (almond meal)
1 teaspoon matcha powder
80 g (3 oz/⅓ cup) cold salted butter, cubed

FRUIT
500 g (1 lb 2 oz/5 cups) grapes (different varieties for colour)
4 apples

Preheat the oven to 180°C (350°F/Gas 4). Put the flour, sugar, ground almonds, matcha powder and butter into a bowl. Rub the butter into the other ingredients rapidly with your fingertips until the mixture resembles breadcrumbs. Chill.

Peel and core the apples, then slice them. Rinse, dry and destalk the grapes. Arrange the fruit in a gratin dish and sprinkle with the crumble. Bake in the oven for approximately 40 minutes, until the crumble is golden.

Ideal serving temperature: warm
Serve with passion fruit ice cream

PEAR AND LEMON CURD
crumble

Preparation: 20 minutes
Cooking time: 20 minutes
Serves 6

CRUMBLE
150 g (5½ oz/1 cup) plain
   (all-purpose) flour
120 g (4½ oz/generous ½ cup)
   unrefined cane sugar
120 g (4½ oz/generous ½ cup)
   cold salted butter, cubed
zest of ½ a lemon

FRUIT
1 kg (3½ oz) firm pears
1 knob of salted butter
4 tablespoons lemon curd

Preheat the oven to 200°C (400°F/Gas 6). Put the flour, sugar, butter and lemon zest into a bowl. Rub the butter into the other ingredients rapidly with your fingertips until the mixture resembles breadcrumbs. Chill.

Peel the pears, quarter them and remove the pips. Melt the butter in a frying pan and brown the pears over medium heat for 5 minutes, or until caramelised. Remove from the heat and add the lemon curd.

Put the pears into 6 small ramekins or a large gratin dish and sprinkle with the crumble. Bake in the oven for approximately 20 minutes, until the crumble is golden.

Ideal serving temperature: cold
No accompaniment necessary

FIG AND WALNUT
crumble

Preparation: 10 minutes
Cooking time: 40 minutes
Serves 6

CRUMBLE
120 g (4½ oz/¾ cup) plain
 (all-purpose) flour
100 g (3½ oz/½ cup) unrefined
 cane sugar
100 g (3½ oz/¾ cup) walnut
 halves, roughly chopped
100 g (3½ oz/scant ½ cup) cold
 salted butter, cubed

FRUIT
800 g (1 lb 12 oz/5 cups) figs
2½ tablespoons honey

Preheat the oven to 180°C (350°F/Gas 4). Rinse and halve the figs.

Put the flour, sugar, walnuts and butter into a bowl. Rub the butter into the other ingredients rapidly with your fingertips until the mixture resembles breadcrumbs. Chill.

Arrange the figs in a gratin dish, drizzle with honey and sprinkle with the crumble. Bake in the oven for approximately 40 minutes, until the crumble is golden.

Ideal serving temperature: warm
Serve with Greek yoghurt

ORANGE AND ALMOND
crumble

Preparation: 20 minutes
Cooking time: 40 minutes
Serves 6

CRUMBLE

150 g (5½ oz/1 cup) plain
   (all-purpose) flour
120 g (4½ oz/generous ½ cup)
   unrefined cane sugar
120 g (4½ oz generous ½ cup)
   cold salted butter, cubed
40 g (1½ oz/½ cup)
   flaked (slivered) almonds

FRUIT

3 oranges
4 clementines
1½ teaspoons vanilla sugar

Preheat the oven to 180°C (350°F/Gas 4). Put the flour, sugar and butter into a bowl. Rub the butter into the other ingredients rapidly with your fingertips until the mixture resembles breadcrumbs. Incorporate the flaked almonds and chill.

Peel the oranges and remove the membranes. Peel the clementines and separate into segments.

Place the citrus segments on a baking tray lined with greaseproof paper (or in a gratin dish). Sprinkle with vanilla sugar and crumble. Bake in the oven for approximately 40 minutes, until the crumble is golden.

Ideal serving temperature: warm
Serve with chocolate ice cream

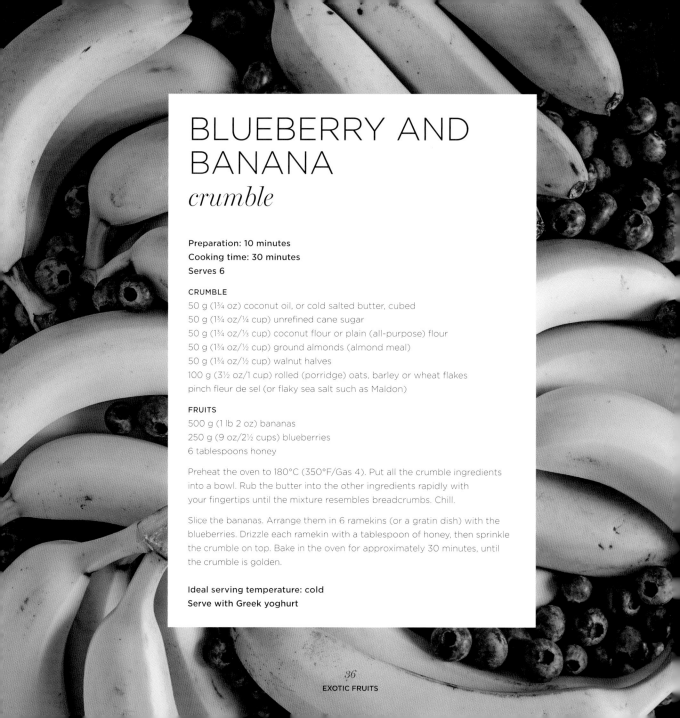

BLUEBERRY AND BANANA
crumble

Preparation: 10 minutes
Cooking time: 30 minutes
Serves 6

CRUMBLE
50 g (1¾ oz) coconut oil, or cold salted butter, cubed
50 g (1¾ oz/¼ cup) unrefined cane sugar
50 g (1¾ oz/⅓ cup) coconut flour or plain (all-purpose) flour
50 g (1¾ oz/½ cup) ground almonds (almond meal)
50 g (1¾ oz/½ cup) walnut halves
100 g (3½ oz/1 cup) rolled (porridge) oats, barley or wheat flakes
pinch fleur de sel (or flaky sea salt such as Maldon)

FRUITS
500 g (1 lb 2 oz) bananas
250 g (9 oz/2½ cups) blueberries
6 tablespoons honey

Preheat the oven to 180°C (350°F/Gas 4). Put all the crumble ingredients into a bowl. Rub the butter into the other ingredients rapidly with your fingertips until the mixture resembles breadcrumbs. Chill.

Slice the bananas. Arrange them in 6 ramekins (or a gratin dish) with the blueberries. Drizzle each ramekin with a tablespoon of honey, then sprinkle the crumble on top. Bake in the oven for approximately 30 minutes, until the crumble is golden.

Ideal serving temperature: cold
Serve with Greek yoghurt

MANGO AND PINEAPPLE
crumble

Preparation: 20 minutes
Cooking time: 40 minutes
Serves 6

CRUMBLE
150 g (5½ oz/1 cup) plain (all-purpose) flour
100 g (3½ oz/½ cup) unrefined cane sugar
120 g (4½ oz/½ cup) cold salted butter, cubed
30 g (1 oz/½ cup) coconut flakes

FRUITS
500 g (1 lb 2 oz) fresh mango or frozen mango
1 small pineapple
1½ teaspoons vanilla sugar

Preheat the oven to 180°C (350°F/Gas 4). Put the flour, sugar and butter into a bowl. Rub the butter into the other ingredients with your fingertips until the mixture resembles breadcrumbs. Incorporate the coconut flakes and chill.

Cut the mango on either side of the stone, then cut or scoop out the flesh. Alternatively, use frozen mango as it comes. Peel the pineapple, cut it into quarters lengthways, then into large triangles. Arrange the fruit pieces in a gratin dish or on a baking tray lined with greaseproof paper, sprinkle with vanilla sugar and the crumble mix. Bake in the oven for approximately 40 minutes, until the crumble is golden.

Ideal serving temperature: warm
Serve with coconut ice cream

DARK CHOCOLATE
crumble

Preparation: 25 minutes
Cooking time: 40 minutes
Serves 6

CRUMBLE

100 g (3½ oz/⅔ cup) plain
   (all-purpose) flour
120 g (4½ oz/generous ½ cup)
   cold salted butter, cubed
50 g (1¾ oz/½ cup) rolled
   (porridge) oats
50 g (1¾ oz/½ cup) ground
   hazelnuts
80 g (2¾ oz/⅓ cup) unrefined
   cane sugar

CHOCOLATE CREAM

200 ml (7 fl oz) single
   (pouring) cream
250 g (9 oz) dark chocolate,
   chopped
1 egg, plus 2 egg yolks
200 ml (7 fl oz) evaporated milk

Preheat the oven to 120°C (230°F/Gas ½). Put the crumble ingredients into a bowl. Rub the butter into the other ingredients rapidly with your fingertips until the mixture resembles breadcrumbs. Chill.

Gently heat the cream in a small saucepan. As it comes to the boil, remove from the heat and add the chocolate. Leave to melt for 5 minutes without stirring.

Beat the egg and yolks together in a bowl.

While stirring, add the evaporated milk to the chocolate and cream. Pour this mixture over the eggs, stirring continuously.

Divide the mixture between 6 ramekins (filled halfway) and place the ramekins on a baking tray. Sprinkle them with the crumble mixture and bake in the oven for approximately 40 minutes. Then brown under the grill for 5 minutes, until the crumbles are golden. Leave to cool to room temperature then chill in the fridge.

Ideal serving temperature: cold
No accompaniment necessary

PEAR AND CHOCOLATE
crumble

Preparation: 15 minutes
Cooking time: 40 minutes
Serves 6

CRUMBLE

100 g (3½ oz/⅔ cup) plain
  (all-purpose) flour
80 g (2¾ oz/⅓ cup) unrefined
  cane sugar
50 g (1¾ oz/½ cup) ground
  hazelnuts
1 tablespoon cocoa powder
60 g (2 oz/¼ cup) cold salted
  butter, cubed

FRUIT

4 large ripe pears (1 kg/2 lb 3 oz)
1 knob of salted butter, cut into
  small cubes
50 g (1¾ oz) dark chocolate,
  chopped

Preheat the oven to 180°C (350°F/Gas 4). Put the flour, sugar, ground hazelnuts, cocoa powder and butter into a bowl. Rub the butter into the other ingredients rapidly with your fingertips until the mixture resembles breadcrumbs. Chill.

Peel and core the pears then slice them finely or cut into small chunks.

Arrange the pears in a gratin dish, dot with small cubes of butter followed by the chocolate and sprinkle with the crumble. Bake in the oven for 40 minutes, until the crumble is golden.

Ideal serving temperature: cold
No accompaniment necessary

CHERRY AND CHOCOLATE
crumble

Preparation: 15 or 25 minutes
Cooking time: 30 minutes
Serves 6

CRUMBLE

120 g (4½ oz/¾ cup) plain
   (all-purpose) flour
100 g (3½ oz/scant ½ cup) cold
   salted butter, cubed
80 g (2¾ oz/⅓ cup) unrefined
   cane sugar
50 g (1¾ oz/⅓ cup) pistachios,
   roughly chopped

FRUIT

1 kg (2 lb 3 oz/5 cups) fresh or
   frozen cherries
60 g (2 oz/½ cup) cornflour
   (cornstarch)
200 g (7 oz) white chocolate,
   broken into large pieces

Preheat the oven to 180°C (350°F/Gas 4). Put the flour, butter, sugar and pistachios into a bowl. Rub the butter into the other ingredients rapidly with your fingertips until the mixture resembles breadcrumbs. Chill.

If using fresh cherries, rinse and remove their stones, or use frozen cherries as they are.

Arrange the fruit in the bottom of 6 ramekins and sprinkle with cornflour. Top with the chocolate pieces, followed by the crumble. Bake in the oven for about 30 minutes, until the crumbles are golden.

Ideal serving temperature: warm
Serve with Greek yoghurt

CLASSIC PARMESAN
crumbles

Preparation: 20 minutes
Cooking time: 20 minutes
Serves 6

CRUMBLE

180 g (6½ oz/1¼ cups) plain
   (all-purpose) flour
160 g (5½ oz/⅔ cup) cold salted
   butter, cubed
40 g (1½ oz/⅓ cup) grated
   Parmesan
1 egg
80 g (2¾ oz/¾ cup) ground
   hazelnuts for winter version
   or ground almonds (almond
   meal) for summer

WINTER VERSION

1 kg (2 lb 3 oz) butternut squash
   (pumpkin)
2 shallots, thinly sliced
1 knob of salted butter
2 pinches of ground nutmeg
freshly ground black pepper

SUMMER VERSION

1 tablespoon olive oil
1 onion, thinly sliced
300 g (10½ oz) spinach leaves
1 knob of salted butter, cubed
350 g (12½ oz/2⅓ cups) fresh or
   frozen peas
200 g (7 oz) goat's cheese,
   cubed
12 mint leaves, snipped
freshly ground black pepper

Preheat the oven to 200°C (400°F/Gas 6). Put the flour, butter, Parmesan, egg and ground nuts into a bowl. Rub the butter into the other ingredients rapidly with your fingertips until the mixture resembles breadcrumbs. Chill.

WINTER CRUMBLE WITH BUTTERNUT SQUASH

Peel the butternut squash, cut it in half, remove the seeds and cut the flesh into small cubes. Cook in a pan of boiling water for 15 minutes, until tender. Drain and mash the butternut squash in the bottom of a gratin dish, then mix in the shallots, butter, nutmeg and pepper. Sprinkle the crumble mix on top and bake in the oven for approximately 20 minutes, until the crumble is golden. Serve hot.

SUMMER CRUMBLE WITH PEAS

Heat the oil in a frying pan and sauté the onion for 5 minutes. Add the spinach and allow to wilt for approximately 2 minutes. Take off the heat. Put the butter, peas, spinach and onion mixture, goat's cheese and mint in a gratin dish and add the pepper. Sprinkle the crumble mixture on top and bake in the oven for approximately 20 minutes, until the crumble is golden. Serve hot.

CARAMELISED
TOMATO
crumble

Preparation: 25 minutes
Cooking time: 50 minutes
Serves 6

CRUMBLE
200 g (7 oz/2⅔ cups) plain (all-purpose) flour
100 g (3½ oz/scant 1 cup) finely grated Parmesan
1 teaspoon chilli powder
freshly ground black pepper
200 g (7 oz/generous ¾ cup) cold salted butter, cubed

FILLING
800 g (1 lb 12 oz) cherry tomatoes
4 onions, thinly sliced
2 teaspoons sugar
2 tablespoons olive oil

Preheat the oven to 200°C (400°F/Gas 6). Put the flour, Parmesan, chilli powder, pepper and butter into a bowl. Rub the butter into the other ingredients rapidly with your fingertips until the mixture resembles breadcrumbs. Chill.

Arrange the tomatoes and onions at the bottom of a gratin dish, sprinkle with sugar, drizzle with oil, then bake in the oven for 30 minutes. Remove from the oven, sprinkle with the crumble mixture and return to the oven for a further 20 minutes, until the crumble is golden.

SPINACH AND RICOTTA

crumble

Preparation: 20 minutes
Cooking time: 30 minutes
Serves 6

CRUMBLE
50 g (1¾ oz/scant ¼ cup) cold salted butter, cubed
180 g (6½ oz/1¼ cups) plain (all-purpose) flour
1 egg
50 g (1¾ oz/⅓ cup) pine nuts
1 teaspoon thyme
freshly ground black pepper

FILLING
500 g (1 lb 2 oz) spinach leaves
2 tablespoons olive oil
2 large yellow onions
250 g (9 oz/1 cup) ricotta
pinch of ground nutmeg
pinch of salt
freshly ground black pepper

Preheat the oven to 200°C (400°F/Gas 6). Put all the crumble ingredients into a bowl and rub the butter into the other ingredients rapidly with your fingertips until the mixture resembles breadcrumbs. Chill.

Rinse and drain the spinach. Heat the oil in a frying pan and sauté the onions until soft. Add the spinach and allow to wilt, then stir in the ricotta, nutmeg, salt and pepper. Spread the mixture in a gratin dish. Sprinkle the crumble on top and bake in the oven for approximately 30 minutes, until the crumble is golden.

COURGETTE AND CASHEW
crumble

Preparation: 20 minutes
Cooking time: 30 minutes
Serves 6

CRUMBLE
150 g (5½ oz/1 cup) plain
  (all-purpose) flour
1 teaspoon ground coriander
1 teaspoon curry powder
1 teaspoon chilli powder
freshly ground black pepper
120 g (4½ oz/generous ½ cup)
  cold salted butter, cubed
120 g (4½ oz/¾ cup) cashews,
  roughly chopped

FILLING
1 tablespoon olive oil
2 onions, thinly sliced
4 courgettes (zucchini), cubed
200 ml (7 fl oz) coconut cream
  or coconut milk
1 tablespoon curry powder
salt and freshly ground black
  pepper

1 bunch of fresh coriander
  (cilantro), chopped, to serve

Preheat the oven to 180°C (350°F/Gas 4). Put the flour, spices and butter into a bowl. Rub the butter into the other ingredients rapidly with your fingertips until the mixture resembles breadcrumbs. Stir in the cashews and chill.

Heat the oil in a flameproof casserole dish, then fry the onions for 5 minutes. Add the courgettes and continue cooking for 5 minutes, stirring regularly. Add the coconut cream, curry powder, salt and pepper, and simmer for 5 minutes.

Sprinkle the courgette mixture with the crumble. Put the casserole dish in the oven for approximately 30 minutes, until the crumble is golden. Serve with the fresh coriander.

CAULIFLOWER CHEESE
crumble

Preparation: 20 minutes
Cooking time: 30 minutes
Serves 6

CRUMBLE
50 g (1¾ oz/scant ¼ cup) cold
   salted butter, cubed
50 g (1¾ oz/scant ¼ cup) soft
   goat's cheese
1 egg
180 g (6½ oz/1¾ cups) plain
   (all-purpose) flour
freshly ground black pepper

FILLING
500 g (1 lb 2 oz) cauliflower
   florets (approximately
   ½ cauliflower)
1 tablespoon olive oil
1 knob of butter
1 teaspoon ground cumin
1 teaspoon paprika
200 ml (7 fl oz) single
   (pouring) cream
250 g (9 oz/1 cup) soft goat's
   cheese, cut into small cubes

Preheat the oven to 200°C (400°F/Gas 6). Put the butter, goat's cheese, egg, flour and pepper into a bowl. Rub the butter into the other ingredients rapidly with your fingertips until the mixture resembles breadcrumbs. Chill.

Rinse the cauliflower florets. Heat the oil and butter in a frying pan and sauté the cauliflower with the paprika and cumin for 5 minutes.

Spread the cauliflower in a gratin dish or on a baking tray lined with greaseproof paper. Drizzle with the cream, sprinkle with the goat's cheese and top with the crumble. Bake in the oven for approximately 30 minutes, until the crumble is golden. Serve hot.

AUBERGINE AND CHICKPEA
crumble

Preparation: 40 minutes
Cooking time: 35 minutes
Serves 6

FILLING

2 medium aubergines
    (eggplants)
350 g (12½ oz/2⅓ cups) cherry
    tomatoes, halved
400 g (14 oz) tinned chickpeas
    (garbanzo beans), drained
    and rinsed
50 g (1¾ oz/⅓ cup) raisins
2 tablespoons olive oil

CRUMBLE

80 ml (2½ fl oz) olive oil
150 g (5½ oz/1 cup) plain
    (all-purpose) flour
2 tablespoons sesame seeds
1 tablespoon sugar
pinch of ground cumin
pinch of ground cinnamon
pinch of ground coriander
pinch of chilli powder

12 mint leaves, snipped, to serve

Preheat the oven to 200°C (400°F/Gas 6). Rinse and cut the aubergines into rounds. Spread them on a baking tray lined with greaseproof paper. Put in the oven for approximately 30 minutes, until golden.

Put all the crumble ingredients into a bowl and rub the butter into the other ingredients rapidly with your fingertips until the mixture resembles breadcrumbs. Chill.

When the aubergines are done, take them out of the oven and add the cherry tomatoes, chickpeas and raisins. Drizzle with oil and sprinkle with the crumble. Bake in the oven for approximately 35 minutes, until the crumble is golden. Serve sprinkled with snipped mint.

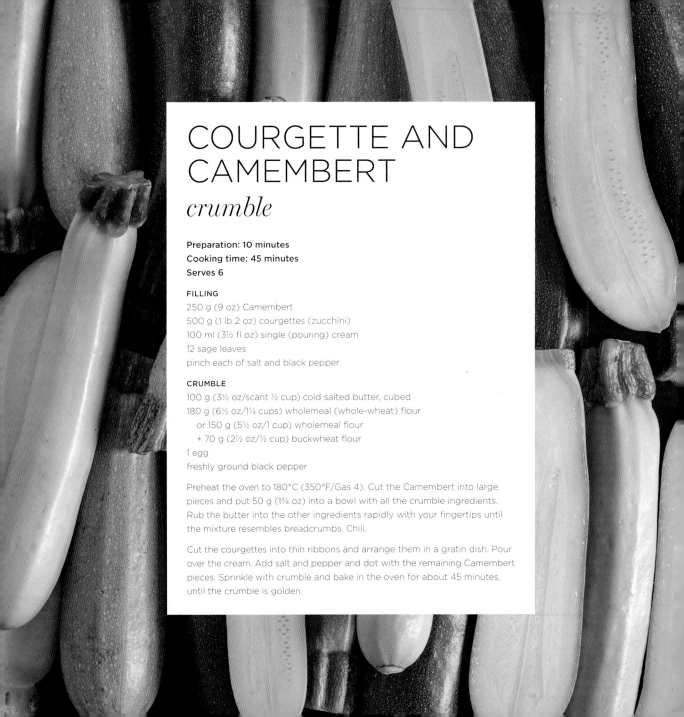

COURGETTE AND CAMEMBERT

crumble

Preparation: 10 minutes
Cooking time: 45 minutes
Serves 6

FILLING
250 g (9 oz) Camembert
500 g (1 lb 2 oz) courgettes (zucchini)
100 ml (3½ fl oz) single (pouring) cream
12 sage leaves
pinch each of salt and black pepper

CRUMBLE
100 g (3½ oz/scant ½ cup) cold salted butter, cubed
180 g (6½ oz/1¼ cups) wholemeal (whole-wheat) flour
   or 150 g (5½ oz/1 cup) wholemeal flour
   + 70 g (2½ oz/½ cup) buckwheat flour
1 egg
freshly ground black pepper

Preheat the oven to 180°C (350°F/Gas 4). Cut the Camembert into large pieces and put 50 g (1¾ oz) into a bowl with all the crumble ingredients. Rub the butter into the other ingredients rapidly with your fingertips until the mixture resembles breadcrumbs. Chill.

Cut the courgettes into thin ribbons and arrange them in a gratin dish. Pour over the cream. Add salt and pepper and dot with the remaining Camembert pieces. Sprinkle with crumble and bake in the oven for about 45 minutes, until the crumble is golden.

APPLE AND BRUSSELS SPROUT
crumble

Preparation 40 minutes
Cooking time: 20 minutes
Serves 6

CRUMBLE
150 g (5½ oz/1 cup) plain (all-purpose) flour
1 egg
freshly ground black pepper
50 g (1¾ oz) Cheddar, cubed
60 g (2 oz) cold salted butter, cubed
100 g (3½ oz/⅔ cup) hazelnuts

FILLING
1 kg (2 lb 3 oz) Brussels sprouts, trimmed and outer leaves discarded
500 g (1 lb 2 oz) apples, peeled, cored and sliced
200 g (7 oz) smoked streaky bacon, chopped
2 tablespoons butter
50 g (1¾ oz) Cheddar, to serve

Preheat the oven to 180°C (350°F/Gas 4). Put the flour, egg, pepper, Cheddar and butter in a bowl. Rub the butter into the other ingredients rapidly with your fingertips until the mixture resembles breadcrumbs. Incorporate the hazelnuts and chill.

Blanch the Brussels sprouts in a pan of boiling water for 3 minutes. Drain, refill the pan with fresh water and bring back to the boil. Boil the sprouts for 15 minutes. Arrange the apples and bacon in a gratin dish. Dot with butter and cheese, then sprinkle with the crumble. Bake in the oven for about 20 minutes, until the crumble is golden. Before serving, grate a generous helping of Cheddar over the dish while still piping hot.

COD AND HAZELNUT
crumble

Preparation: 45 minutes
Cooking time: 30 minutes
Serves 6

FILLING

1 kg (2 lb 3 oz) potatoes
100 ml (3½ fl oz) milk
2 tablespoons butter
pinch of grated nutmeg
2 pinches of salt
freshly ground black pepper
8 basil leaves, finely chopped
300 g (10½ oz) cod fillets or
   loins, cut into large cubes

CRUMBLE

50 g (1¾ oz/⅓ cup) plain
   (all-purpose) flour
2 tablespoons cold salted
   butter, cubed
25 ml (¾ fl oz) olive oil
2 crackers, roughly crumbled
50 g (1¾ oz/generous ⅓ cup)
   hazelnuts, roughly chopped
1 garlic clove, chopped

Peel the potatoes and cook them in a pan of boiling water for 30 minutes until tender. Mash them and beat in the milk, butter, nutmeg, salt, pepper and chopped basil.

Preheat the oven to 180°C (350°F/Gas 4). Put the flour, butter, oil and crackers into a bowl. Rub the butter into the other ingredients rapidly with your fingertips until the mixture resembles breadcrumbs. Add the hazelnuts and garlic, and stir in gently. Chill.

Spread the mashed potato on the bottom of a gratin dish. Top with the chunks of cod and sprinkle with crumble. Bake in the oven for approximately 30 minutes, until the crumble is golden.

SALMON AND WATERCRESS
crumble

Serves 6
Preparation: 20 minutes
Cooking time: 20 minutes

CRUMBLE
90 g (3 oz/scant ⅔ cup) plain (all-purpose) flour
60 g (2 oz/½ cup) grated Parmesan
freshly ground black pepper
75 g (2¾ oz/scant ⅔ cup) cold salted butter, cubed

FILLING
1 knob of butter
2 shallots, thinly sliced
½ bunch of watercress, chopped
3 skinless salmon fillets, cut in half
200 ml (7 fl oz) double (heavy) cream
½ bunch of dill, chopped
pinch of salt
freshly ground black pepper

Preheat the oven to 200°C (400°F/Gas 6). Put the flour, Parmesan, pepper and butter in a bowl. Rub the butter into the other ingredients rapidly with your fingertips until the mixture resembles breadcrumbs. Chill.

Melt the butter in a frying pan and gently fry the shallots for 5 minutes. Add the watercress and cook for 2 minutes. Combine the cream, dill; salt and pepper in a bowl. Arrange the salmon in a gratin dish, top with the watercress cream and sprinkle with the crumble. Bake in the oven for approximately 15–20 minutes, until the crumble is golden. Serve hot.

DUCK AND SWEET POTATO
crumble

Preparation: 40 minutes
Cooking time: 30 minutes
Serves 6

CRUMBLE

120 g (4½ oz/¾ cup) plain
  (all-purpose) flour
freshly ground black pepper
100 g (3½ oz/scant ½ cup) cold
  salted butter, cubed
60 g (2 oz/⅔ cup) walnut halves
60 g (2 oz/⅓ cup) grapes

FILLING

1 kg (2 lb 3 oz) sweet potatoes
100 ml (3½ fl oz) double
  (heavy) cream
salt and freshly ground black
  pepper
4 thighs of duck confit
6 sprigs of parsley, chopped

Preheat the oven to 180°C (350°F/Gas 4). Put the flour, pepper and butter into a bowl. Rub the butter into the other ingredients rapidly with your fingertips until the mixture resembles breadcrumbs. Stir in the walnuts and grapes. Chill.

Peel the sweet potatoes, cut into thick rounds and steam or boil them in a pan for 30 minutes, until tender. Mash the sweet potatoes. Add the cream and beat to form a purée. Season with salt and pepper.

Remove and discard the skin and bones from the duck confit. Shred the meat with a fork.

Divide the purée between 6 ramekins, add the duck meat and sprinkle with the crumble. Bake in the oven for approximately 30 minutes, until the crumbles are golden. Serve sprinkled with chopped parsley.

SAUSAGE, LEEK AND COMTÉ
crumble

Preparation: 20 minutes
Cooking time: 25 minutes
Serves 6

CRUMBLE

120 g (4½ oz/¾ cup) plain
  (all-purpose) flour
freshly ground black pepper
50 g (1¾ oz/½ cup) grated
  Comté
80 g (2¾ oz/⅓ cup) cold salted
  butter, cubed

FILLING

3 leeks, white parts only
1 knob of salted butter
1 tablespoon olive oil
1 shallot, chopped
6 chipolata sausages
salt and freshly ground
  black pepper
200 ml (7 fl oz) single
  (pouring) cream
150 g (5½ oz 1½ cups) grated
  Comté

Preheat the oven to 200°C (400°F/Gas 6). Put the flour, pepper, Comté and butter into a bowl. Rub the butter into the other ingredients rapidly with your fingertips until the mixture resembles breadcrumbs. Chill.

Rinse the leeks well and cut into I cm (½ in) sections. Heat the butter with the oil in a frying pan, then cook the leeks and shallot gently for 5 minutes. Season with salt and pepper.

Arrange the chipolatas in a gratin dish. Cover with the leeks. Drizzle with cream, sprinkle with the Comté and top with the crumble. Season with salt and pepper. Bake in the oven for approximately 25 minutes, until the crumble is golden.

CHICKEN AND GORGONZOLA
crumble

Preparation: 30 minutes
Cooking time: 40 minutes
Serves 6

CRUMBLE
125 g (4½ oz/¾ cup) plain
  (all-purpose) flour
freshly ground black pepper
50 g (1¾ oz) Gorgonzola
80 g (2¾ oz/⅓ cup) cold salted
  butter, cubed

FILLING
250 g (9 oz) parsnips
250 g (9 oz) leftover roast
  chicken (or 2 cooked
  chicken thighs)
2 sticks of celery with leaves
250 g (9 oz) Gorgonzola,
  cut into large chunks
2 tablespoons mustard
250 ml (8½ fl oz) single
  (pouring) cream
freshly ground black pepper

Preheat the oven to 180°C (350°F/Gas 4). Put the flour, pepper, Gorgonzola and butter into a bowl. Rub the butter into the other ingredients rapidly with your fingertips until the mixture resembles breadcrumbs. Chill.

Peel the parsnips and cut them into thin rounds. Shred the chicken with your fingers or a fork, and discard any bones or skin. Set aside the celery leaves, and cut the sticks into small 5 mm (¼ in) sections.

In a gratin dish, mix the parsnips, chicken, celery, Gorgonzola and mustard. Add the cream and pepper, and sprinkle with the crumble. Bake in the oven for approximately 40 minutes, until the crumble is golden. Serve with snipped celery leaves.

ACKNOWLEDGEMENTS

For my Ninouche. Later on we will make crumbles together.
They may be the first dessert you cook like a grown-up!
Thank you to Akiko for your patience.
Thank you to Quentin for your patience and advice.
Thank you to Chi-E San for tasting all these crumbles.
Thank you, Maman, for giving me so much encouragement.

Crumbles by Sabrina Fauda-Rôle

First published in 2016 by Hachette Books (Marabout)
This English hardback edition published in 2017
by Hardie Grant Books

Hardie Grant Books (UK)
52-54 Southwark Street
London SE1 1UN
hardiegrant.co.uk

Hardie Grant Books (Australia)
Ground Floor, Building 1
658 Church Street
Melbourne, VIC 3121
hardiegrant.com.au

ISBN: 978-1-78488-126-9

Design: Frédéric Voisin
Editing: Anne Guerquin and Natacha Kotchetkova

For the English hardback edition:

Publisher: Kate Pollard
Senior Editor: Kajal Mistry
Editorial Assistant: Hannah Roberts
Publishing Assistant: Eila Purvis
Translation: Gilla Evans
Copy editing: Kate Wanwimolruk
Typesetter: David Meikle
Colour Reproduction by p2d

Printed and bound in China by 1010

10 9 8 7 6 5 4 3 2 1